TOOLS FOR CAREGIVERS

- **F&P LEVEL:** D
- **WORD COUNT:** 22
- **CURRICULUM CONNECTIONS:** animals, habitats, nature

Skills to Teach

- **HIGH-FREQUENCY WORDS:** are, become, frogs, in, they, up, water
- **CONTENT WORDS:** bugs, croak, eat, eggs, grow, jump, swim, tadpoles
- **PUNCTUATION:** exclamation point, periods
- **WORD STUDY:** long e, spelled ea (eat); long o, spelled oa (croak); long o, spelled ow (grow); compound word (tadpoles)
- **TEXT TYPE:** information report

Before Reading Activities

- Read the title and give a simple statement of the main idea.
- Have students "walk" though the book and talk about what they see in the pictures.
- Introduce new vocabulary by having students predict the first letter and locate the word in the text.
- Discuss any unfamiliar concepts that are in the text.

After Reading Activities

This books introduces the frog life cycle. Draw or show readers a frog life cycle diagram. Explain to readers that frogs are amphibians. They often lay eggs in water. Tadpoles are born in water with tails and gills. As they grow, their tails shrink and they develop legs. They also form lungs so they can breathe on land. Have each reader draw the life cycle of a frog. Can they think of other animals that have a unique life cycle?

Tadpole Books are published by Jump!, 5357 Penn Avenue South, Minneapolis, MN 55419, www.jumplibrary.com

Copyright ©2020 Jump. International copyright reserved in all countries. No part of this book may be reproduced in any form without written permission from the publisher.

Editor: Jenna Trnka **Designer:** Michelle Sonnek

Photo Credits: Michiel de Wit/Shutterstock, cover; Tony Campbell/Shutterstock, 1; Jay Ondreicka/Shutterstock, 2tl, 3; Ivan Kuzmin/Alamy, 2mr, 4–5; age fotostock/SuperStock, 2tr, 6–7; Clara Bastian/Shutterstock, 2ml, 8–9; PRILL/Shutterstock, 2br, 10–11; Terry Whittaker Wildlife/Alamy, 2bl, 12–13; Eric Isselee/Shutterstock, 14–15; Ivan Kuzmin/Shutterstock, 16.

Library of Congress Cataloging-in-Publication Data
Names: Nilsen, Genevieve, author.
Title: Frogs / by Genevieve Nilsen.
Description: Tadpole edition. | Minneapolis, MN: Jump!, Inc., (2020) | Series: Backyard animals | Audience: Age 3–6. | Includes index.
Identifiers: LCCN 2019016661 (print) | LCCN 2019017977 (ebook) | ISBN 9781645270980 (ebook) | ISBN 9781645270966 (hardcover: alk. paper) | ISBN 9781645270973 (paperback)
Subjects: LCSH: Frogs—Juvenile literature.
Classification: LCC QL668.E2 (ebook) | LCC QL668.E2 N55 2020 (print) | DDC 597.8—dc23
LC record available at https://lccn.loc.gov/2019016661

ANIMALS

OGS

by Genevieve Nilsen

TABLE OF CONTENTS

tadpole
books

WORDS TO KNOW

croak

eat

eggs

jump

swim

tadpoles

FROGS

Frogs croak.

Frogs jump.

bug

Frogs eat bugs.

eggs

**Frog eggs
are in water.**

tadpole

◀ ┈┈┈┈

Frog eggs become tadpoles!

Tadpoles swim.

They grow up.

LET'S REVIEW!

What is this frog doing?

INDEX

They grow up.

LET'S REVIEW!

What is this frog doing?

INDEX